MW01100947

Life Skills

Conflict Resolution

Communication, Cooperation, Compromise

by Robert Wandberg, PhD

Consultants:
Roberta Brack Kaufman, EdD
Dean, College of Education
Concordia University
St. Paul, Minnesota

Millie Shepich, MPH, CHES
Health Educator and District Health Coordinator
Waubonsie Valley High School
Aurora, Illinois

LifeMatters
an imprint of Capstone Press
Mankato, Minnesota

Thank you to Heather Thomson of BRAVO Middle School, Bloomington, Minnesota; to Christine Ramsay of Kennedy High School, Bloomington, Minnesota; and especially to all of their students, who developed the self-assessments and provided many real stories.

LifeMatters Books are published by Capstone Press
PO Box 669 • 151 Good Counsel Drive • Mankato, Minnesota 56002
http://www.capstone-press.com

Printed in the United States of America

Library of Congress Cataloging-in-Publication Data

Wandberg, Robert.
    Conflict resolution: Communication, cooperation, compromise / by Robert Wandberg.
        p.   cm. — (Life skills) *series*
    Includes bibliographical references and index.
    ISBN 0-7368-0695-4 (hardcover) — ISBN 0-7368-8836-5 (softcover)
    1. Teenagers—United States—Social Conditions—Juvenile literature. 2. Teenagers—United States—Life skills guides—Juvenile literature. 3. Violence—United States—Juvenile literature. 4. Conflict management—United States—Juvenile literature. [1. Conflict management. 2. Life skills. 3. Violence.] I. Title.
    HQ796 .W243 2000
    303.6'9'0835—dc21   00-035232
                                                                     CIP

    Summary: Defines conflict, some of its effects, and how teens can deal with conflict, including violence, rape, and murder. Includes self-assessments to help teens judge how well they deal with conflict.

Staff Credits

Charles Pederson, editor; Adam Lazar, designer; Katy Kudela, photo researcher

Photo Credits

Cover: UPmagazine/©Tim Yoon
International Stock/©Patrick Ramsey, 35; ©Peter Langone, 39
Photo Network, 48/©Grace Davies, 7; ©Myrleen Cate, 23; ©Esbin-Anderson, 57
Unicorn Stock Photos/©Jeff Greenberg, 59
Uniphoto/©Bob Daemmrich Photos, Inc., 11; ©Melanie Carr, 16; ©Llewellyn, 28, 34, 54; ©William B. Folsom, 31; ©Caroline Woodham, 44; ©Paul Conklin, 47
UPmagazine/©Tim Yoon, 5, 15, 25, 33, 43, 51

Table of Contents

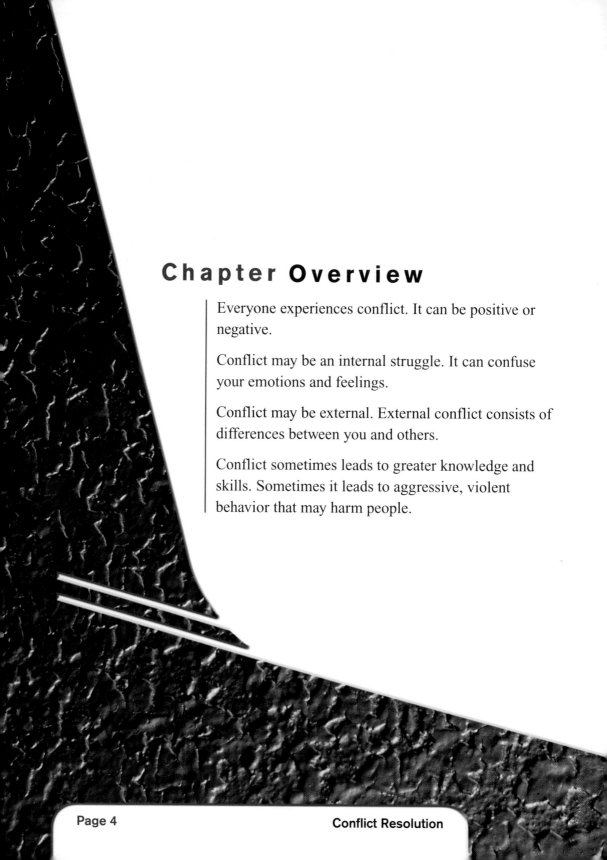

Chapter Overview

Everyone experiences conflict. It can be positive or negative.

Conflict may be an internal struggle. It can confuse your emotions and feelings.

Conflict may be external. External conflict consists of differences between you and others.

Conflict sometimes leads to greater knowledge and skills. Sometimes it leads to aggressive, violent behavior that may harm people.

Conflict Resolution

CHAPTER 1

✿

The Nature of Conflict

It may seem that conflict is everywhere. You may feel swamped with wars, crimes, and arguments. The good news is that you are not powerless. In this chapter you will learn about these **ConflictMatters.** You also will take a self-assessment to see how you cope with conflict.

Defining Conflict

Conflicts are disagreements or struggles. Most people think conflict is only negative or even violent. But there can be positive conflict. For example, a sports contest is a conflict, but it usually has a positive result. Win or lose, the players may have more knowledge or self-awareness afterward.

What is the correct definition of *conflict*: battle, clash, war, competition, contest, disagreement, fight, match, duel, dispute? (Answer: All of these words are appropriate definitions.)

The reality is that conflict is usually more negative than positive. Negative conflict can lead to high-risk behavior and harm a person's health. When it's uncontrolled, conflict can lead to devastating, even deadly, violence. This book will examine negative conflict and how to deal with it.

What Is Conflict Resolution?

Conflict can be serious, but its effects may be reduced through conflict resolution. This is the process of reducing and calming conflicts so that no violence occurs. Violence is words or actions that are intended to harm people or their property. It can be as annoying or troublesome as a threat or as deadly as murder. Violence also includes vandalism, or intentional harm to someone's property. For example, graffiti—illegally drawing or writing on a public surface—is vandalism.

Violence can change people's attitude toward their privacy, rights, and freedom. It can cause people not to trust others. It may make people feel afraid, nervous, and confused. Conflict resolution is one way to build or recapture trust in relationships.

The main reason to learn and practice conflict resolution skills is to prevent conflict from becoming violent. Having a better understanding of violence will help you prevent dangerous situations. The more you know, the better you can protect yourself and others from violence. Conflict resolution also can lead to cooperation among people, which is usually better than being in conflict.

Lifestyle and Conflict

Many teens experience painful conflict. Conflict can occur from actions we take. For example, someone may push another person while waiting in a line. The person who was pushed may react by yelling or pushing back. Along with our actions, our lifestyle choices can lead to conflict. Lifestyle includes the everyday behaviors people choose. The Centers for Disease Control and Prevention (CDC) identifies six lifestyle areas. Poor choices in these areas contribute to most of the deaths, illness, and injury among young people. The areas are:

- Tobacco use

- Alcohol and other drug use

- Sexual behaviors resulting in HIV infection, other sexually transmitted diseases (STDs), sexually transmitted infections (STIs), or unplanned pregnancy

Unhealthy eating patterns

Lack of exercise

Behaviors that result in intentional or unintentional injury. Suicide, or killing oneself, and murder are examples of intentional injuries. Car crashes and drowning are examples of unintentional injuries.

The two main kinds of conflict are internal and external conflict. Each of the CDC's six lifestyle areas could cause these kinds of conflict. Let's look at each kind.

Internal Conflict

Internal conflicts are a person's struggles with himself or herself. Internal conflicts can be intense. Many internal conflicts for teens revolve around the CDC's lifestyle areas. You have to resolve some of these conflicts quickly. You can take more time for other conflicts and use appropriate decision-making skills. Internal conflicts may involve wondering what's best in a situation.

For example, suppose you notice suicide warning signals in your best friend. Should you ignore the signals or try to get help? Other examples of internal conflict might include whether to:

Start smoking

Try alcohol or other drugs at a party

Have sexual intercourse with a person you have been dating

Lose 10 pounds

Try out for a school sports team

External Conflict

External conflict occurs between people. To some degree, conflict occurs in most relationships. This is because all people have their own values, skills, personalities, and opinions. People rarely agree on all aspects of their relationship.

External conflict may involve only two people. For example, you may not want to cheat on a test. Yet a friend wants you to give him the answers. Conflict also can involve small or large groups. For example, gangs might have conflict over drugs or territory. Large groups such as countries may have conflict in the form of wars. Issues people feel strongly about such as religion or politics may cause conflict.

Simple conflict between two people sometimes leads to violence. For example, you might feel angry and ready to fight if someone roughly said, "Get out of my way." Sometimes a person may use not words but a gesture. Conflict may start as an insult about appearance, race, religion, or culture. However, conflict does not have to lead to violence.

Life is full of conflicts. When you can, choose the ones you want to deal with. It's often best to avoid or get away from conflicts when your health or safety are at stake. Dealing with conflicts while they are still small is smart. Internal or external conflicts that start out small can turn nasty over time.

Ally, Age 16

The party was going strong. Ally was sitting in the kitchen with a group of students from her school. Jake, from Ally's geometry class, produced a bottle of gin. He stated the rules for a drinking game he wanted to play. Ally was having fun and didn't want to leave. However, seeing the alcohol, she began to feel uncomfortable. She decided to leave and thought it would be easier now before the game started. "I have to get home," she announced and got up to leave. "My mom gets on my case when I'm late. See you at school on Monday."

Conflict Resolution

Self-Assessments and Conflict

Self-assessments are tests that can give us information to help us know ourselves better. There are many kinds of self-assessments. Often, teen self-assessments are about relationships. Other common topics include risk of heart disease, cancer, or mental illness. Topics may include attitudes toward issues such as the death penalty or birth control. Schools may provide self-assessments to help students choose a career.

Periodically assessing yourself can help you keep track of what is normal for you. It also can help you see how you change over time. The key to self-assessments is that *you* interpret the information, not someone else.

Try the following self-assessment. The teens who developed it believe the items are important regarding peaceful conflict resolution.

Conflict Resolution: A Teen Self-Assessment

Read items 1–15 below. On a separate sheet of paper, write the number that best describes you. Use this rating scale:

1 = Never	2 = Sometimes	3 = Always

	1	2	3
1. I recognize that violent behavior is a threat.	1	2	3
2. I know how to face a conflict.	1	2	3
3. I can recognize an abusive relationship.	1	2	3
4. I know how to keep a conflict peaceful.	1	2	3
5. I refuse to fight physically.	1	2	3
6. I know how to stop fights.	1	2	3
7. I encourage others to refuse to fight.	1	2	3
8. I can control my anger.	1	2	3
9. I ask for help with conflicts I can't solve.	1	2	3
10. I know how to tell others when I am angry.	1	2	3
11. I avoid using weapons.	1	2	3
12. I can negotiate, or discuss, with others to solve conflicts.	1	2	3
13. I avoid using alcohol and other drugs.	1	2	3
14. I resist peer pressure that may lead to conflict.	1	2	3
15. I know how to calm myself down.	1	2	3

Add up your points. The closer you are to 45, the better you probably are at coping with conflict. If you scored 3 on any items, that's great. Did you score 1 or 2 on any items? You can work to develop those skills.

"I was eating lunch with Gabe. Otis, who's a real jerk, comes over and says to Gabe, 'Hey Blackbelt Boy, you going to eat that?' Then he sticks his thumb in Gabe's sandwich. Gabe takes martial arts lessons, and I think Otis wanted to fight him. I expected Gabe to get up and kick Otis's butt. I know he could, 'cause I've faced him in practice, and he's good. But Gabe finished the rest of his lunch, then we left. Otis insulted him all the way down the hall, but Gabe ignored him. That was pretty good. Most people would worry what everyone would think, so they'd fight back."—Arthur, age 18

Points to Consider: ConflictMatters

How can conflict be viewed as positive?

Give examples of internal and external conflict.

What is the main purpose of conflict resolution?

Based on the self-assessment, which items would be the easiest for you to improve? How could you improve?

Chapter Overview

Maslow's hierarchy helps to explain human behavior.

When facing a conflict, a person must know appropriate ways to deal with it.

People resolve conflict by ignoring it, avoiding it, confronting it, or resolving it.

Calming yourself or others might include exercising, being alone, or talking the problem out.

CHAPTER 2

Conflict:
The Unavoidable
Experience

Angelique, Age 14

Angelique was having a terrible day. When she woke up with a pimple, she had hoped no one would notice. "Nice zit," was the first comment she heard at school. Then she heard someone make fun of her shorts and T-shirt. She thought she heard someone snickering about her nose, which Angelique already thought was huge.

As we wake every morning, often we can see how the day will go. Some days are positive, and we feel good about ourselves. However, sometimes our days are terrible. Maybe you got teased when your voice squeaked during a speech. Perhaps people called your sister names because of the way she looks.

These comments hurt and can make a person feel bad. You can't stop others from saying hurtful things, but you have the power to stop listening! You can let those negative message fly by you like the leaves on a windy day. The **ResolutionMatters** presented in this chapter are healthy ways to solve conflict and prevent violence.

Maslow's Hierarchy

Abraham Maslow was an American psychologist who developed a hierarchy describing people's needs. A hierarchy shows the order or importance of something. Maslow's hierarchy shows that five needs motivate people in this order:

1. **Physical needs:** having food, warmth, water, sleep, shelter

2. **Safety needs:** being protected from harm, crime, and the environment

3. **Belonging needs:** having friends and relationships, being able to give and receive affection

4. **Self-esteem needs:** feeling valued and worthwhile, respecting self and others; having self-confidence

5. **Self-actualization:** achieving goals, fulfilling dreams and unique potentials

When people can't meet these needs, conflict may occur. Imagine that two starving people see one piece of food. They may have a conflict about who gets the food. If the people are hungry enough, the conflict might even lead to physical violence.

As you have read, one of Maslow's needs is for safety. Try the following quiz to see how safe you are.

Read items 1–35 below. On a separate sheet of paper, write the number following each item that describes you best. Use this rating system:

1 = Never	2 = Sometimes	3 = Always

Home Safety

1. Do you lock your doors and windows?	1	2	3
2. Do you make your house look as though someone is there when you're away?	1	2	3
3. Do you keep jewelry and other valuable items out of sight?	1	2	3
4. Do you keep only small sums of money at home?	1	2	3
5. Do you keep strangers out of your home?	1	2	3
6. Do your doors have peep-holes so you can see out without someone seeing in?	1	2	3
7. Do you stay away if you come home and find a door or window unexpectedly open?	1	2	3
8. Do you keep keys away from anyone who may duplicate them? Examples include people who park cars or workers inside your home.	1	2	3
9. Do you avoid hiding keys in obvious places such as under a doormat?	1	2	3

School Safety

10. Do you keep your locker combination to yourself?	1	2	3
11. Do you follow bus safety rules?	1	2	3
12. Do you avoid having chemicals and weapons?	1	2	3
13. Do you avoid stealing?	1	2	3

Conflict Resolution

14. Do you avoid sexual harassment of other students? That is, you don't do or say sexual things to others who may not welcome them.	1	2	3
15. Do you avoid religious harassment of other students?	1	2	3
16. Do you avoid racial or cultural harassment of other students?	1	2	3
17. Do you avoid harassment based on someone's sex or sexual orientation?	1	2	3
18. Do you avoid harassing people with physical or mental disabilities?	1	2	3
19. Do you avoid fighting?	1	2	3
20. Do you report other students' suspicious behavior to school staff?	1	2	3

Street Safety

21. Do you walk with confidence?	1	2	3
22. Are you alert to what is going on around you?	1	2	3
23. Do you walk with friends or in a group?	1	2	3
24. Do you stay in well-lighted areas and avoid lonely areas?	1	2	3
25. Are you alert when people stop you for directions or other information?	1	2	3

26. Do you go to the nearest house or store if you believe you are being followed? 1 2 3

27. Do you scream if you are in trouble? For example, do you yell "help" or "fire" to attract help? 1 2 3

Car Safety

28. Do you lock car doors and windows, especially when you leave your car unattended? 1 2 3

29. Do you park in well-lighted areas? 1 2 3

30. As the driver or passenger, are you aware of how much gas is in the tank? 1 2 3

31. If there is a flat tire, do you drive or ride to a safe area to change it? 1 2 3

32. If your car stalls, do you stay in the car? 1 2 3

33. Do you ask strangers to call the police instead of allowing them to help you? 1 2 3

34. Do you honk the car horn if you feel threatened? 1 2 3

35. Do you avoid giving rides to strangers? 1 2 3

The higher your score (105 possible), the more safety precautions you are following. Items you scored 1 or 2 on show areas in which you may be creating potentially dangerous situations.

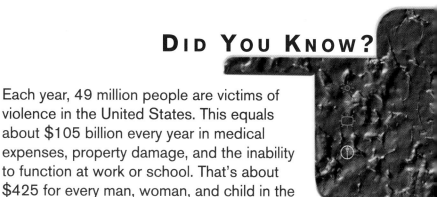

Each year, 49 million people are victims of violence in the United States. This equals about $105 billion every year in medical expenses, property damage, and the inability to function at work or school. That's about $425 for every man, woman, and child in the United States.

Uncontrolled Conflict

The bad news is that violence does occur. The good news is that it's preventable! An honest look at violence can strengthen our wisdom, skills, and conflict-reducing behaviors.

Violence can occur anywhere. It may occur in homes, schools, places of worship, recreation areas, and workplaces. It often occurs without warning, which can make it hard to resolve conflicts. However, by learning conflict resolution skills, we may resolve differences respectfully without violence.

Dealing With Conflicts

As a conflict enters our life, we have to decide how to deal with it. Sometimes the decision has to be made immediately. For example, your friend asks you to sneak him a hamburger while you're working for a restaurant. In other cases, we may have several hours, even days or weeks, to deal with the conflict. For example, you've been saving your money to buy a car. Your parents, however, think you should use the money for college or technical school.

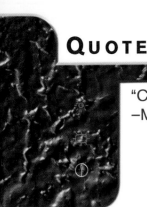

"Conflict is inevitable, but combat is optional."
—Max Lucado, writer

When a conflict does occur, we have four options.

Ignore. Do whatever it takes to disregard a conflict.

Avoid. Do whatever it takes to escape a conflict.

Confront. Do whatever it takes to win a conflict.

Resolve. Do whatever it takes to negotiate and settle a conflict. This often means both sides win.

The first three options often make one side the loser. By resolving the conflict, both sides can win. Far too often, though, conflicts end in violence.

Anger Management

Everyone gets angry at times. Uncontrolled anger sometimes leads to violence. When anger is out of control, you or others may be physically harmed in the short term. Long-term, or chronic, anger can increase your risk of high blood pressure. Chronic anger may harm your heart or lungs.

Learning to control anger is a big step in dealing with conflict. Some people calm down by vigorous exercise. For example, a person may run, walk fast, or participate in aerobic classes. Others may calm down by being alone. Still others seek another person to talk with. Talking about their anger helps them to control it.

The bottom line is to control your anger. What works for one person may not work for everyone. Find the way that works best for you. Then, do whatever it takes to calm your anger and avoid harming yourself, others, or property.

Points to Consider: ResolutionMatters

Which of Maslow's needs do you think is the basis of most conflicts among teens? Why?

List as many quiet places as possible where you could go to be alone and think things out.

List as many people as possible with whom you could talk when you are angry.

Choose three items you scored low on in the safety quiz. How could you increase your safety in those areas?

Chapter Overview

Crime reports tell us the number and types of crimes that are committed. They also describe where or when the crime occurs.

These same reports also identify something about the offender and the victim.

A self-assessment can help you become aware of your risk for violence.

The number of murders reported annually has declined recently. However, some situations signal greater concern for safety.

Violent behavior leading to murder is linked to many factors. These include gang activity and drugs.

Conflict Resolution

CHAPTER 3

☼

Violence:
The Ultimate Conflict

Crime in the streets. Violence in the media. Everywhere you look, you might feel scared by what you see. It might seem impossible to remain safe in today's world. Knowing something about crime and your risk of violence can help you practice **SafetyMatters.**

A violent crime occurs every 18 seconds in the United States. This includes:

• One physical attack every 29 seconds

• One armed robbery every 54 seconds

• One rape every 5 minutes

• One murder every 24 minutes

Violent crime also occurs in Canada, though at a lower rate than in the United States.

Violence Happens

Violence does occur. However, the more you know about crime and violence, the better you can protect yourself and others. Your knowledge may help you to prevent and reduce the amount and severity of crime and violence.

Where and When Are Crimes Committed?

Crimes can occur anywhere. Still, it's possible to make some general statements about crime. More crimes occur in urban areas than in the suburbs. With more people around in a city, criminals may feel less noticed. More crimes occur in the suburbs than in the country.

Overall, most crimes occur on Saturday evenings between 8:00 P.M. and 2:00 A.M. However, robberies of homes tend to occur during weekdays, especially when people are at work.

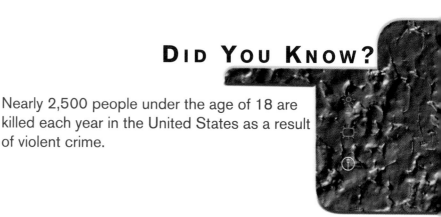

Did You Know?

Nearly 2,500 people under the age of 18 are killed each year in the United States as a result of violent crime.

Who Is the Violent Offender?

It is difficult to say who commits most violent crimes. No one description fits all offenders, or criminals. However, the Federal Bureau of Investigation's (FBI) Uniform Crime Report notes:

Young men under age 25 commit most violent crime.

Many offenders were abused as children.

About 40 percent of people in prison have family members who have been in prison.

Most violent offenders in prison report having used drugs.

About 28 percent of male prisoners completed high school. This compares with 85 percent of all men ages 20–29.

Who Are the Victims?

Being a victim of a crime usually happens without warning. It's often scary to read the statistics about how many people may become a crime victim.

Many victims of violent crime have a background similar to the offenders. Far more males are both victims and offenders. The lower the income, the greater the risk for being a victim. Teens and young adults are more likely than older people to be victims.

Barry, Age 15

Barry was watching the TV news. The first few stories were about some crime being committed. That happened all the time. Every time he heard a story like this, Barry became more scared. He began to think it might be a good idea to move somewhere else. The mountains sounded good to him.

What's My Risk for Violence?

Read items 1–12 below. On a separate sheet of paper, write the number that best describes you. Use this rating scale:

1 = Never   2 = Rarely   3 = Sometimes   4 = Often

1. Do you hang around with gang members?	**1**	**2**	**3**	**4**
2. Do you damage other people's property for fun?	**1**	**2**	**3**	**4**
3. Could you get a gun easily?	**1**	**2**	**3**	**4**
4. Do you carry a gun, knife, or other weapon for protection?	**1**	**2**	**3**	**4**
5. Do you use alcohol?	**1**	**2**	**3**	**4**
6. Do you use other illegal drugs?	**1**	**2**	**3**	**4**
7. Do you threaten to hurt people?	**1**	**2**	**3**	**4**
8. Do you beat up people?	**1**	**2**	**3**	**4**
9. Do you participate in group fights?	**1**	**2**	**3**	**4**
10. Do you steal things?	**1**	**2**	**3**	**4**
11. Do you skip school?	**1**	**2**	**3**	**4**
12. Do you get in trouble with the police or other authorities?	**1**	**2**	**3**	**4**

Add up your points. The closer your score is to 48, the higher your risk of violent conflict is. If your score was high, you still can reduce your risk. If your score was low, great job! Keep supporting nonviolent behaviors in yourself, your family, and your friends.

In 1990, New York City had 2,262 murders. It experienced 629 murders in 1998.

Homicide

Homicide is another word for murder. Everywhere you look, homicide might seem to be on the rise. In reality, several large U.S. cities had a falling homicide rate during the 1990s. These cities included New York, Baltimore, Boston, Dallas, Detroit, Houston, Philadelphia, and Washington, D.C. There seem to be several reasons for this.

The population is becoming older, especially the baby boomers. They are now mostly in their 40s and early 50s.

There is more community involvement in crime prevention.

The use of illegal drugs like crack and cocaine is decreasing.

Some experts note that homicide rates are falling partly because fewer young people are joining gangs. Rising employment and tougher policing also may have contributed to lower homicide rates.

Two main causes of homicide are gang violence and illegal drug use. These two causes often are related. Although homicide victims range in age from babies to senior citizens, most are young men. Shootings, beatings, and stabbings are the most common homicide causes. Other causes of homicide include arson and drowning. Arson is a fire intentionally started to destroy property.

According to the Bureau of Justice, younger homicide victims are likely to know their killer. In the last 20 years, on average more than half of victims from babies to age 19 knew their killer.

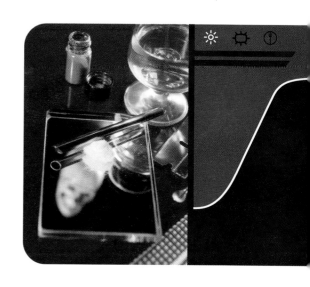

Alcohol, Drugs, and Conflict

In more than half of all homicides, the victim, killer, or both were drunk or on other drugs. There is a close relationship between violence and alcohol and other drugs. However, no definite evidence shows that alcohol and drugs cause crime. Some people believe that many offenders first decide to commit their crime. Then they use alcohol or other drugs for courage and confidence. Either way, alcohol and other drugs are often the deciding factor in whether violence occurs.

Points to Consider: SafetyMatters

Why do you think most crimes are committed on weekends or at night?

How do you think violence threatens your health? How does it threaten the health of the general population?

Do you agree with the reasons given for why the U.S. homicide rate is declining? Explain.

What are the two main reasons for homicide?

Chapter Overview

Family conflict is the cause of much violence. Abuse can occur in families of all descriptions.

Guns in the home are a leading cause of death and injury in the home. This may be intentional or accidental injury.

A relationship may exist between the amount of violence on TV and the amount of violence at home. There are ways to reduce the amount of violence.

Child abuse includes physical, sexual, and emotional abuse.

CHAPTER 4 ☼

Families and Conflict

FamilyMatters can be a source of resolving conflict or making it worse. In this chapter you will become aware of the risks at home or in the community associated with behaviors that might lead to violence.

Family Conflict

Families have changed a lot over the years. Many of our parents or grandparents grew up during the 1950s, 1960s, and 1970s. Many popular TV series of that time showed traditional families. These families had a working father, a stay-at-home mother, and two children. Today, only about 10 percent of all families fit that description. The families of today are:

Nuclear: mother, father, and children (biological or adopted)

Extended: nuclear family plus relatives such as grandparents, aunts, uncles, or cousins

Single parent: one parent who is unmarried, divorced, separated, or widowed; someone is widowed when the husband or wife dies.

Blended: families from remarriage; the nonbiological spouse is called a stepparent.

Mixed: unique organizations such as unmarried couples living together, with or without children

Luis, Age 13

Luis, his two brothers, and his two half-sisters live with Luis's mother and stepfather. That many people in a three-bedroom house means little privacy for anyone. Luis likes the weekends he stays at his biological father's house, because he gets a bedroom to himself. Still, Luis likes his stepfamily okay.

Recently, Luis's best friend, Aaron, asked if he could stay at Luis's house awhile. Aaron and his stepmother fight a lot, and Aaron felt she didn't want him around. "Lots of kids live in families like mine," says Luis. "I'm just lucky we all get along. It could be a lot worse."

It's possible for all these different kinds of families to be healthy. The opposite of a healthy family is a dysfunctional family, which can't or won't meet its members' needs. These include physical needs, safety and security needs, social needs, and self-esteem or emotional needs.

Some families can't adequately feed the children. Some families can't keep the children safe and secure. Many families can't provide for children's social, mental, and emotional needs. In fact, children may be neglected or abused. Neglect and abuse are very serious.

Did You Know?

Male teens are more likely to die from the use of firearms than from all natural causes of death combined.

Abuse Within a Family

Family conflict and violence occur among people of all races and religions. It occurs among the wealthy and the poor.

Women and children are commonly victims of family violence. Between two and four million women are reported as battered, or beaten up, every year in the United States. Such beating is a form of physical abuse. Nearly two million children are reported as battered. Many experts believe the actual number is much higher because a large number of cases are unreported. Canadian officials believe that as many as two out of three cases of family abuse remain unreported.

Guns in the Home

Many things cause violence. One major part in the occurrence of violence at home is the presence of a gun. With a gun in the home, a person is eight times more likely to kill someone or be killed. If a family fight occurs and someone has a gun, a person is twelve times more likely to be killed.

The Center to Prevent Handgun Violence reports these causes of gun-related deaths among young people:

18 percent—fights over guns or drugs

15 percent—feuds or long-term disagreements

13 percent—accidents while playing with or cleaning guns

12 percent—romantic quarrels

10 percent—fights over personal property

32 percent—other

Guns at home don't automatically result in violence. Most people use guns responsibly for hunting or other sports. Because guns are dangerous, however, they require special handling. They should be stored unloaded and locked in a gun case. The ammunition should be stored apart from the guns.

TV and Conflict

The American Psychological Association (APA) reports that U.S. schoolchildren watch 8,000 TV murders by sixth grade. They also see 100,000 other acts of TV violence in the same period. By age 18, the typical teen has seen on TV 250,000 violent acts, 40,000 murders, and 800 suicides. About 66 percent of adults believe there is a relationship between violence on TV and crime.

Children most likely to be aggressive are those who watch more violent programs than other types. They may believe that these programs show life as it is. They also may identify strongly with aggressive characters. TV violence also may reinforce the violence that is found in a child's everyday life.

Surveys show that many children feel that fighting back is important. This may be due to what they see in the movies and on TV. You are not powerless. You can help change TV for the better.

If you watch a violent TV program with someone, talk about the causes and consequences of that violence.

If you don't like the violence you see, write a letter to the producer of the show or its advertisers. Tell them what you didn't like.

Start a letter-writing campaign to protest violence on TV.

Friends may try to talk you into seeing a violent movie. Stand your ground and don't go if you think it's too violent. Suggest a different movie that everyone is comfortable seeing.

Object to programs that promote hate toward groups or individuals.

Child Abuse

Some people falsely believe only dirty, creepy men harm children and youth. In reality, fathers, mothers, brothers, sisters, aunts, uncles, grandparents, and neighbors can cause serious harm to young people. Harm to children and youth is extremely disturbing.

A common form of violence is child abuse. This mistreatment puts a child's physical or emotional health at risk. It kills more than 1,000 children each year. Nearly half of these children are under one year of age. There are several forms of abuse:

Neglect means that the family fails to provide for the basic needs of the person. This includes other neglectful behavior, such as not feeding or properly caring for a child.

Physical abuse is when a person harms another person physically. Common abuse signs include scratches, bumps, bruises, burns, and broken bones and teeth.

Sexual abuse is sexual behavior between an adult and a young person or child. It can involve inappropriate touching, showing or taking pictures, and having sexual intercourse. Both males and females can be victims of sexual abuse.

Emotional abuse is when a parent or other caregiver uses words or feelings to embarrass or shame a child. For example, constant criticism and put-downs are emotional abuse: "You can't do anything right!" Emotional abuse includes exposing a child to violence against someone else, such as when parents hit each other. More than 3 million children in the United States witness spouse abuse each year. These children may develop emotional difficulties, depression, and problems in school.

Abuse often runs in families. Many parents relate to their own children in the same ways their parents related to them. If their parents abused them, they are likely to abuse their own children.

Education is a huge part of reducing child abuse. Often, parents who abuse never learned a better way to treat their children. By attending a parenting class, parents can learn healthy, loving ways to treat their children. It may be hard, but the circle of conflict leading to family violence can be broken.

Points to Consider: FamilyMatters

Do you believe the availability of handguns is connected to violence? Explain.

Look at the Fast Fact at the top of page 37. What are examples of gun-related deaths that could fit in the category "other"?

Do you think there is a relationship between watching TV and violence? Why or why not?

Why do you think child abuse runs in families?

Many cases of child abuse are unreported. Why do you think that's true?

Chapter Overview

Rape is a violent crime against another person and can happen to anyone. It's about power over someone.

Rape can have long-term physical and emotional effects.

Date and acquaintance rape occur between people who know each other. These are the most common kinds of rape.

After a rape, victims can take several steps to recover.

Reducing rape is the responsibility of both males and females.

CHAPTER 5

⌗

Rape

You may not believe that you or someone you know could be raped. However, rape occurs more often than most people believe. In this chapter, you'll learn about rape. The suggestions in this chapter also can help you avoid becoming a victim of this violent act. Reducing the violence of rape involves **DefenseMatters.**

Rape Is a Crime of Violence

Rape is when one person forces another to engage in sexual intercourse. Experts agree that power, anger, and aggression—*not* sexual desire—drive rape. The effects of a rape can last months, years, or even a lifetime. Surviving rape's effects is the most important thing. Preventing the conflict of rape is important, as well.

Rape can happen to people of all ages, including men and boys. Rape victims range in age from infants to senior citizens. Males are victims in about 5 percent of all rape cases. Females ages 16 to 24 are two to three times more likely to be raped than younger or older females.

Some rapes are not physically violent. Victims may not fight back because they are afraid. However, it's still rape if the victim is unwilling.

Statutory rape is another type of rape. It is sexual intercourse with a person who is younger than a state's age of consent. This is the age at which a person is considered an adult and able to make his or her own decisions about sex. Age of consent varies from state to state. Even if a person agrees to sex, it is rape if the person is not of legal age.

The Effects of Rape

The effects of rape are enormous and can't be understated. Victims may be seriously injured, infected with an STD (including HIV), or become pregnant. Recovery from the physical results of a rape can take a long time.

The emotional effects of a rape can be even more disturbing and painful. They may last longer than the physical effects. Rape victims may lose trust in others. They may feel angry at themselves or the rapist. Many rape victims experience sleeplessness, crying, anxiety, depression, headaches, nightmares, and sexual problems. Some victims have decreased appetite. Others develop eating disorders.

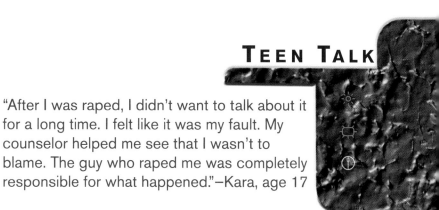

"After I was raped, I didn't want to talk about it for a long time. I felt like it was my fault. My counselor helped me see that I wasn't to blame. The guy who raped me was completely responsible for what happened."–Kara, age 17

Date and Acquaintance Rape

Most rapists are not strangers to their victims. People known to the victim commit about 80 percent of rapes. *Acquaintance rape* is the term given to this type of rape. The acquaintance may be a relative, neighbor, classmate, or coworker. *Date rape* occurs when a rapist (usually a male) forces his date to have sexual intercourse during a date.

Females and males both can help prevent date rape. For females:

Be assertive and communicate directly with your date about your sexual limits.

Be conscious of the nonverbal messages you are sending.

Be alert to situations where you're open to rape.

Be aware of "date-rape drugs" such as Rohypnol ("roofies"). These drugs may be put into a victim's drink to cause him or her to pass out.

Don't accept drinks (with or without alcohol) from strangers.

Don't leave your drink unattended at a party. If you have left a drink, get a fresh one from someone you know and trust.

Stay in control. Don't use any alcohol or other drugs.

Trust your instincts. If a situation feels wrong, it probably is. Leave the situation.

Date and acquaintance rape are common for several reasons:

The victim trusts the attacker.

The victim may not realize right away what's happening.

The victim might not want to fight back for fear of embarrassment.

The victim, attacker, or both were using alcohol or other drugs.

For males, it doesn't matter:

If your date looks "sexy"

If you have a condom

If your date is on the pill

If you spend a lot of money on the date

If your date gives you a sexy kiss or a big hug

If you have had sex with your date on other occasions

Where you are

How long you've been dating

It does matter if your date says no. To force someone into sexual intercourse is rape! The rapist can control his or her behavior and is fully responsible for the rape.

After a Rape

In those awful moments after a rape, a victim may wish only to forget what happened. Yet, hard as it is, dealing with the rape can start the healing process. If you or someone you know is raped, following are some things to know.

The rape is *never* the victim's fault.

Call 9-1-1 for emergency medical care and police. Be sure to tell all medical personnel what has happened. They need the information to care for you properly. They also need to check for possible injuries, sexually transmitted diseases and HIV, and pregnancy.

Don't wash, comb your hair, or change your clothes. Your hair, hands, fingernails, skin, face, sex organs, and clothes contain a great deal of evidence.

Remember as many details as possible about the rapist's appearance, car, or clothing. This will help the police.

Get counseling to deal with your feelings. Many medical and police services have specially trained staff to deal with sexual assaults. They also can direct you to a counseling service.

Call a sexual assault or crisis hot line for advice and services.

Consider pressing charges against your attacker. A social worker can tell you what will happen if you do.

Reducing Rape

Unfortunately, not everyone agrees on how to stop a rapist. It seems that victims who resist their rapist may stop the rape. However, they also may increase their chance of being injured.

Many people take self-defense courses to protect themselves. They may install home security systems or lock car and house doors and windows. They may stay away from dark areas and never pick up hitchhikers (female or male).

The attitudes children learn in their families seem to be especially important in how they view sexual violence. Many rapists are from unloving, jealous, or abusive families.

Families can help reduce the number of rapes by being open about sexuality. Honestly communicating and having caring and respectful relationships are equally important.

Families are not the only place where people learn attitudes. Some experts suggest that sports, the media, even cartoons may contribute to violent attitudes. Society's expectations of males and females, and attitudes about who should begin sexual activity, may be a factor. Studies in this area are not conclusive.

Other influences include the community, businesses, medicine, law, education, counseling, and religious groups. Education about rape is also important in stopping it. Encourage your school and community to offer educational programs about rape.

MYTH VS. FACT

Myth: If a female goes somewhere to be alone with a male, she wants to have sex.

Fact: Two people can be alone with each other for many reasons that have nothing to do with sex. Unless both people are of legal age and agree to have sex, it is a crime.

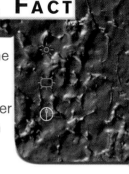

Murry, Age 19

Murry hadn't thought much about rape. In fact, he joked about it sometimes with his friends. Then his next-door neighbor was raped after school. She wouldn't talk with any males. This concerned Murry, who decided to do something about it. "I didn't rape her, but I can understand her feelings toward men and our attitudes. Men cause most rape, so I think men need to help stop it. I can't believe I ever joked about raping someone."

Points to Consider: DefenseMatters

Is there a best way to fight rape? Explain.

Why do you think states have laws against statutory rape?

Why might rape victims be angry at themselves afterward?

Why do you think it's important for a rape victim not to shower or change clothes?

Do you think that males are important in stopping rape? Explain.

Chapter **Overview**

All relationships involve some amount of conflict. It's important to learn to resolve conflict in healthy ways.

A self-assessment can help you learn about your attitudes toward relationships.

Communication is vital in avoiding sexual and family conflicts.

Peer mediation is one way many schools help to decrease the levels of violence.

CHAPTER 6

⌖

Building a
Healthy Future

This chapter focuses on conflict resolution and peer mediation skills. These skills can be used when people experience difficulties in a relationship. **RelationshipMatters** are built on a basic need to belong.

Conflict Occurs

We often accept minor disagreements among friends. But too often we expect perfection from that special person in our life. Expecting perfection in oneself or others is unreasonable and can be unhealthy.

We like to spend time with people we care about. We like to share goals, dreams, ideas, and values. This open and honest communication is the foundation for healthy relationships. However, even in the best relationships, disagreements occur.

Here's the breakdown of how married couples originally met:

Through mutual friends: 35 percent

By introducing themselves: 32 percent

Through family members: 15 percent

By being classmates, coworkers, neighbors: 13 percent

Other ways: 5 percent

Conflict doesn't mean the couple shouldn't be together. It simply means they need to communicate what they want. Healthy relationships are made up of people who can compromise and resolve conflicts in a positive manner. Conflict can be a sign that the people are thinking for themselves.

Even couples married for many years often say they have had serious disagreements. A common word of wisdom from these couples is never to end the evening angry. That is, talk about and resolve conflicts early, before they become big. That's a basic idea.

Healthy relationships are wonderful. However, they don't happen by themselves. They take work. The following self-assessment can gauge your attitudes toward the work needed for a healthy relationship.

Are You Willing to Have a Healthy Relationship?

Read items 1–13 below. On a sheet of paper, write the number that best describes your attitude. Use this rating scale as you circle the numbers.

1 = Never	2 = Sometimes	3 = Always

	1	2	3
1. I will be open-minded in the relationship. I won't insist that my way is the best.	1	2	3
2. I will spend quality time in the relationship.	1	2	3
3. I will work hard to solve relationship problems.	1	2	3
4. I will share the chores and duties of the relationship.	1	2	3
5. I will share in making important relationship decisions.	1	2	3
6. I will use good communication skills.	1	2	3
7. I will be helpful.	1	2	3
8. I will trust and care for my partner.	1	2	3
9. I will be honest with my partner.	1	2	3
10. I will be committed to the relationship.	1	2	3
11. I will accept the differences between me and my partner.	1	2	3
12. I will share the power in the relationship.	1	2	3
13. I will share my values, thoughts, opinions, and feelings with my partner.	1	2	3

Add up your score. The closer you are to 39 points, the more likely you'll have healthy relationships. For items with a 1 or 2, don't worry. These are simply areas to practice communicating and compromising.

Avoiding Sexual Conflict

Be clear about communicating your sexual boundaries, or what you are willing to do.

Avoid riding with strangers or groups of people you have just met.

Learn how to and practice saying no.

Be especially alert in unfamiliar areas.

Stay sober.

Encourage your school to offer sexual violence prevention programs.

Resolving Family Conflicts

All families have conflicts from time to time. Conflict may involve parenting, finances, schooling, and many other things. Healthy families often have the following characteristics to help them resolve conflicts:

Mutual respect. Family members value and respect what is worthwhile and important to other members.

Specified responsibilities. All family members contribute to the family by performing specific duties, tasks, and responsibilities.

Communication is critical to healthy relationships. You want to get your message across. At the same time, you don't want to embarrass, criticize, or hurt the other person's feelings. Here are five guidelines for a healthy relationship:

1. **Stop:** Take time to calm yourself. Taking deep breaths often helps a person relax.

2. **Think:** Decide why you or the other person might be angry.

3. **Talk:** Calmly say what you want or need. Focus on your own feelings without accusing the other person. Don't say, "You always take my stuff without asking." Instead, you might calmly say, "I get angry when you take my stuff without asking. I feel like you don't care about what I want."

4. **Listen:** Ask what the other person wants or needs. Remain calm.

5. **Act:** Figure out how to make things right. Think of a way that both people can keep their pride.

Good communication skills. The family creates a safe and supportive atmosphere to share feelings, emotions, and information. This is vital for effective communication.

Shared values. Family members have common goals and beliefs about what's important.

Emotional support for all. Especially in times of stress and disappointment, family members work together to help each other with problems.

Ability to manage change. People leave, babies are born, finances change, family members grow older. Healthy families deal effectively with such change.

Conflict Resolution Skills

When you are resolving conflicts, you can take certain steps to be successful. Here are a few of them.

Stay calm and in control; don't let emotions take over. Take time-outs whenever necessary to calm down.

Keep a positive attitude that a solution can be found.

Try to understand the other side. Both sides want their needs met, so both sides need a clear understanding of each other.

Listen to the other person's side.

Focus on how you feel about the other person's actions. Don't accuse the other person.

Think of as many solutions to the conflict as possible.

Evaluate each possible solution.

Agree on a solution.

Stick to the agreement.

Ask for help if a solution cannot be reached.

Lucinda and Gayle, Age 18

Lucinda and Gayle had a big fight near school. Their friends broke it up and convinced them to go see a peer mediator. The mediator helped them feel like someone cared about their feelings. He helped them work out their problems. Now Lucinda and Gayle get along, even if they aren't exactly friends. They even worked together and got a good grade on a school project.

Peer Mediation

When students have a conflict, they sometimes can resolve it through peer mediation. That's when a person about the same age as those in the conflict mediates, or helps resolve, a conflict. The mediator will require the resolution to be safe, legal, nonviolent, and respectful. The peer mediator typically does the following:

Finds a time and location that's okay with both parties

Remains neutral in the conflict and won't order a solution

Describes the guidelines for the meeting: (1) be truthful; (2) solve your own problem; (3) no put-downs; (4) no name-calling or insults; (5) no threats; (6) no violence; (7) no interrupting; (8) be respectful; (9) follow through on any agreement.

Allows all people to state their side of the conflict

Discusses each side

Helps people think of possible solutions

May offer additional solutions to the conflict

Helps judge each suggested solution

Helps the people choose a solution

Doesn't give up

Negotiates a solution if the people can't decide

Writes down the solution

Has the people sign an agreement

Schedules another meeting to determine how things are going

It is not always easy to find an acceptable resolution to conflicts. Mediation can give students alternatives to violence. The intention is to find a way for all parties to have a positive outcome.

Conflict resolution takes practice. If you stick with it, you likely will become better and better at solving conflicts.

Why do conflicts occur in healthy relationships?

Why do you believe that relationships become unhealthy?

What are several communication guidelines for healthy relationships?

What is the purpose of school peer mediation programs? How do they work? How could you start one in your school?

NOTE

At publication, all resources listed here were accurate and appropriate to the topics covered in this book. Addresses and phone numbers may change. When visiting Internet sites and links, use good judgment.

Internet Sites

Community Police Consortium
www.communitypolicing.org
Information about community policing and special training; provides access to numerous resources, as well as a chat room on community policing.

Partnerships Against Violence Network (PAVNET Online)
www.pavnet.org
Information on violence prevention programs and technical information for states and local communities

Hot Lines

Boys Town Hot Line (females can call, too)
1-800-448-3000
1-800-448-1833 (TDD)

Covenant House Nineline
1-800-999-9999

National Domestic Violence Hot Line
1-800-799-7233 (24 hours a day)

National Youth Crisis Hot Line
1-800-448-4663

For More Information

Useful Addresses

Al-Anon Family Group Headquarters, Inc.
1600 Corporate Landing Parkway
Virginia Beach, VA 23454-5617
www.al-anon.alateen.org
1-800-4AL-ANON (425-2666)

American Trauma Society
8903 Presidential Parkway, Suite 512
Upper Marlboro, MD 20772-2656
1-800-556-7890
www.amtrauma.org

Boys Town USA
13940 Gutowski Road
Boys Town, NE 68010
www.boystown.org

Childhelp USA
15757 North 78th Street
Scottsdale, AZ 85260
1-800-4-A-CHILD (1-800-422-4453)
1-800-222-4453 (TDD)
www.childhelpusa.org

Covenant House
346 West 17th Street
New York, NY 10011
1-800-999-9999
www.covenanthouse.org/kid/kid.htm

National Center for Injury Prevention and
Control (NCIPC)
Mailstop K65
4770 Buford Highway Northeast
Atlanta, GA 30341-3724
www.cdc.gov/ncipc

National Clearinghouse on Child Abuse and
Neglect Information
330 C Street Southwest
Washington, DC 20447
1-800-394-3366
www.calib.com/nccanch

National Coalition Against Domestic Violence
(NCADV)
PO Box 18749
Denver, CO 80218
1-800-799-7233
www.ncadv.org

For Further Reading

Chaiet, Donna, and Francine Russell. *The Safe Zone: A Kid's Guide to Personal Safety.* William
Morrow, 1998.

Gedatus, Gus. *Date and Acquaintance Rape.* Mankato, MN: Capstone, 2000.

Havelin, Kate. *Child Abuse: "Why Do My Parents Hit Me?"* Mankato, MN: Capstone, 2000.

Peacock, Judith. *Anger Management.* Mankato, MN: Capstone, 2000.

anger management (ANG-gur MAN-uhj-muhnt)—the ability to control anger

assertive (uh-SUR-tiv)—able to stand up for yourself and say what you think

compromise (KOM-pruh-mize)—to create a win-win situation by agreeing to give and take

conflict resolution (KON-flikt rez-uh-LOO-shuhn)—the process of reducing and calming conflicts so that no violence occurs

emotional abuse (ee-MOH-shuhn-uhl uh-BYOOSS)—constant verbal criticism, with no feelings of affection or love

homicide (HOM-uh-side)—murder

neglect (nuh-GLEKT)—the disregarding or ignoring of the physical or emotional needs of another

negotiation (nuh-goh-shee-AY-shuhn)—discussing and considering a compromise

peer mediation (PEER mee-dee-AY-shuhn)—a conflict resolution process where a neutral third person assists two or more people in solving a problem

physical abuse (FIZ-uh-kuhl uh-BYOOSS)—bodily harm inflicted on another person

rape (RAYP)—sexual intercourse that is forced on the victim

sexual abuse (SEK-shoo-wuhl uh-BYOOSS)—inappropriate sexual behavior forced upon another by one who is older or in a position of authority

victim (VIK-tuhm)—a person who was wounded or hurt

violence (VYE-uh-luhnss)—words or actions that are meant to harm people or the things they care about

Index

abuse, 12, 27, 35, 36, 38–40, 48
alcohol, 7, 10, 12, 29, 31, 45, 46
American Psychological Association
    (APA), 37
anger, 12, 55
    chronic, 22
    controlling, 22–23
    management, 22
    and rape, 43
appearance, 9, 10, 15, 16
attitudes, 6, 11, 48, 49, 52, 56

boundaries, communicating, 45, 54

calm, 6, 12, 22, 23, 55, 56
Centers for Disease Control and
    Prevention (CDC), 7, 8
Center to Prevent Handgun Violence,
    37
child abuse, 38–40. *See also* abuse
communication. *See* talking
compromise, 52, 53
conflict, 5–8, 12, 17, 36, 37, 40, 51, 52,
    55, 57
    avoiding, 10, 22
    confronting, 22
    coping with, 12
    definition, 5, 6
    external, 9–10
    ignoring, 13, 16, 22
    internal, 8–9, 10
    negotiation, 12, 22
    prevention, 7
    protecting yourself, 7
    resolution, 6, 11, 21, 22, 33, 51, 52,
      54, 56, 57–58
confidence, 19, 31
ConflictMatters, 5

counseling, 47, 48
crime, 5, 17, 18, 25, 26–27, 28, 29–31,
    37
    offenders, 27, 28, 31
    prevention, 30
    victims, 27–28, 30, 31
culture, 10, 19

death, 6, 7, 27, 36, 37, 39
DefenseMatters, 43
disagreements. *See* conflict
drugs, 7, 9, 12, 27, 29, 30, 31, 45, 46

eating patterns, 7, 44
education, 21, 27, 29, 48, 54
emotional abuse, 39. *See also* abuse
exercise, 7, 22

family, 16, 29, 33–40, 48, 54–55
FamilyMatters, 33
feelings, 6, 53, 55, 56, 57. *See also*
    anger
    afraid, 6, 25, 28
    anger, 12, 44, 55
    anxiety, 44
    confused, 6
    depression, 39, 44
    inadequate, 10
    nervous, 6
    uncomfortable, 10
fighting, 6, 10, 12, 19, 29, 36, 37 , 38
friends, 9, 17, 19, 29, 35, 38, 51

gangs, 9, 29, 30
goals, 17, 51, 55
guns. *See* weapons

harassment, 19